How To Use This Study Guide

This five-lesson study guide corresponds to *"Taking Authority Over the Wind and Waves in Your Life" With Rick Renner* (Renner TV). Each lesson in this study guide covers a topic that is addressed during the program series, with questions and references supplied to draw you deeper into your own private study of the Scriptures on this subject.

To derive the most benefit from this study guide, consider the following:

First, watch or listen to the programs prior to working through this study guide. (Programs can also be viewed at **renner.org** by clicking on the Media/Archives links or on our Renner Ministries YouTube channel.)

Second, take the time to look up the scriptures included in each lesson. Prayerfully consider their application to your own life.

Third, use a journal or notebook to make note of your answers to each lesson's Study Questions and Practical Application challenges.

Fourth, invest specific time in prayer and in the Word of God to consult with the Holy Spirit. Write down the scriptures or insights He reveals to you.

Finally, take action! Whatever the Lord tells you to do according to His Word, do it.

For added insights on this subject, it is recommended that you obtain Rick Renner's book *Dressed To Kill: A Biblical Approach to Spiritual Warfare and Armor*. You may also select from Rick's other available resources by placing your order at **renner.org** or by calling 1-800-742-5593.

TOPIC

Attacks When You're on the Brink of a Breakthrough

SCRIPTURES

1. **Ephesians 6:12** — For we wrestle not against flesh and blood, but against principalities, against powers, against the rulers of the darkness of this world, against spiritual wickedness in high places.

2. **Mark 4:35, 37-41** — And the same day, when the even was come, he saith unto them, Let us pass over unto the other side. And there arose a great storm of wind, and the waves beat into the ship, so that it was now full. And he was in the hinder part of the ship, asleep on a pillow: and they awake him, and say unto him, Master, carest thou not that we perish? And he arose, and rebuked the wind, and said unto the sea, Peace, be still. And the wind ceased, and there was a great calm. And he said unto them, Why are ye so fearful? how is it that ye have no faith? And they feared exceedingly, and said one to another, What manner of man is this, that even the wind and the sea obey him?

3. **Mark 5:1-5** — And they came over unto the other side of the sea, into the country of the Gadarenes. And when he was come out of the ship, immediately there met him out of the tombs a man with an unclean spirit who had his dwelling among the tombs; and no man could bind him, no, not with chains Because that he had been often bound with fetters and chains, and the chains had been plucked asunder by him, and the fetters broken in pieces: neither could any man tame him. And always, night and day, he was in the mountains, and in the tombs, crying, and cutting himself with stones.

4. **Matthew 8:28** — And when he was come to the other side into the country of the Gergesenes, there met him two possessed with devils, coming out of the tombs, exceeding fierce, so that no man might pass by that way.

A Note From Rick Renner

I am on a personal quest to see a "revival of the Bible" so people can establish their lives on a firm foundation that will stand strong and endure the test as the end-time storm winds begin to intensify.

In order to experience a revival of the Bible in your personal life, it is important to take time each day to read, receive, and apply its truths to your life. James tells us that if we will continue in the perfect law of liberty — refusing to be forgetful hearers but determined to be doers — we will be blessed in our ways. As you watch or listen to the programs in this series and work through this corresponding study guide, I trust that you will search the Scriptures and allow the Holy Spirit to help you hear something new from God's Word that applies specifically to your life. I encourage you to be a doer of the Word that He reveals to you. Whatever the cost, I assure you — it will be worth it.

Thy words were found, and I did eat them;
and thy word was unto me the joy and rejoicing of mine heart:
for I am called by thy name, O Lord God of hosts.
— Jeremiah 15:16

Your brother and friend in Jesus Christ,

Rick Renner

Taking Authority Over the Wind and Waves in Your Life

Copyright © 2019 by Rick Renner
1814 W. Tacoma St.
Broken Arrow, OK 74012-1406

Published by Rick Renner Ministries
www.renner.org

ISBN 13: 978-1-6803-1601-8

ISBN 13 eBook: 978-1-6803-1639-1

GREEK WORDS

1. "wrestle" — πάλη (*pale*): pictures struggling or fighting; depicts intense combat sports, which included boxers, wrestlers, and pankratists

2. "against" — πρός (*pros*): against; pictures very close contact

3. "principalities" — ἀρχάς (*archas*): those who hold the highest seats of power; high-ranking demon spirits that have held their seats of power since ancient times

4. "powers" — ἐξουσίας (*exousias*): pictures those who have received license to do whatever they wish wherever they desire to do it

5. "rulers of the darkness of this world" — κοσμοκράτορας (*kosmokratoras*): rulers; power that is arranged or disciplined; orderly power and troops

6. "wickedness" — πονηρία (*poneria*): iniquity; pictures something wicked, malevolent, or insidious

7. "there arose" — γίνομαι (*ginomai*): pictures something that takes one off guard or by surprise; something unexpected; to happen (suddenly), or to come into being

SYNOPSIS

The five lessons in this study on *Taking Authority Over the Wind and Waves in Your Life* will focus on the following topics:

- Attacks When You're on the Brink of a Breakthrough
- Why and When Spiritual Attacks Come
- Dealing with Faithless Thoughts When You're Under Attack
- Taking Authority Over the Invisible Realm
- Learning To Exercise Christ-Given Authority

The emphasis of this lesson:

The real problem the disciples faced was not the waves and the water. It was *the wind*. When we are under attack, we need to learn to look beyond the symptoms to *the source* of what is coming against us.

Not Your Ordinary Wrestling Match

The apostle Paul described in vivid detail the picture of the spiritual battle we face. In Ephesians 6:12, he said, "For we wrestle not against flesh and blood, but against principalities, against powers, against the rulers of the darkness of this world, against spiritual wickedness in high places."

The key to understanding this passage is in knowing the meaning of the word "wrestle." In Greek, the word for "wrestle" is *pale*, which means simply *wrestling*. It pictures *struggling or fighting* and depicts *intense combat sports, which included boxers, wrestlers, and pankratists.*

In our western culture, when we hear the word "wrestle," we think of two men in a competition, each trying to pin the other to the mat. In the ancient Greek world, the word "wrestle" (*pale*) carried a much more intense meaning. When the readers of Paul's letter heard the word "wrestle," they would have immediately envisioned certain images in their minds and quickly connected it to another Greek word — the word *palaestra*.

The *palaestra*, or the House of Combat Sports, as it was also known, was a facility found in every major Greek and Roman city. You can still see the ruins of *palaestras* in Athens, Rome, Ephesus, and Pergamum. These were houses of great struggle, conflict, and fighting, and they featured three primary sports.

The Three Sports of the Palaestra

Boxing was the first type of sport that took place in the *palaestra*, but it was not the kind of boxing you might think. It wasn't two men wearing boxing shorts and plump red gloves fastened to their hands. On the contrary, boxing in the Greek and Roman world was much more intense, and its participants predominantly battled it out in the nude.

When boxers fought, they took straps of leather that were 16 feet long and wrapped them around their arms. They started at the elbows, went up the forearms, across the wrists, and around the knuckles. And affixed to the strap around each knuckle was a nail that was serrated like the blade of a knife. When boxers threw their fists furiously against their opponent, they left deep gashes wherever their punches landed. In some cases, they even killed their opponents.

If you look at the decorative vases of the ancient Greeks, they often portray Greek athletic contests. Grotesque images of boxers with missing ears and noses, and even having their eyes gouged out, were commonly displayed. Indeed, it was a blood-spilling sport that was a serious affair — virtually nothing was off limits.

Wrestling was the second type of sport found in the *palaestra*, and as with boxing, wrestling was also conducted in the nude. Again, nothing was off limits. It was an "anything goes" competition. Fingers, arms, and legs were commonly broken. Wrestling at the *palaestra* was a back-snapping, bone-breaking event.

Pankration was the third type of sport featured in the *palaestra*. The word *pankration* is a compound of two Greek words: the word *pan*, which means *all*, and the word *kratos*, which means *power*. When these two words are compounded to form the word *pankration*, it describes *those who were "all-powerful"* — *those who had more power than anyone else.*

Of the three sports of the *palaestra*, *pankration* was the most fierce. Those who participated were called *pankratists*. These were the men who survived the boxing and the wrestling matches. They came into the *pankration* arena armed with clubs that were covered with protruding nails along with satchels filled with rocks. It, too, was a blood-spilling sport.

All of this imagery is tucked away inside the word "wrestle." Those in the First Century who read Paul's letter to the Ephesians would have understood all this. They knew that Paul was describing a very serious conflict with the devil — and just how committed the enemy is to taking us down.

Who We're Really Fighting Against

Looking again at Ephesians 6:12, we read, "For we wrestle not against flesh and blood, but against principalities, against powers, against the rulers of the darkness of this world, against spiritual wickedness in high places."

Five times in this one verse the word "against" is used. It is the Greek word *pros*, which means *against*, and it describes *very close, intimate contact.* It carries the idea of being *face-to-face, shoulder-to-shoulder, ribcage-to-ribcage.* Paul uses this word to help us understand that the spiritual conflict is not just happening to Christians serving as missionaries in foreign countries. The fight is real, and it will come very close to each of us at some point in our lives.

Paul also mentioned four different groups of evil forces we are up against.

The **first** is "principalities." This is the Greek word *archas*, and it describes *those who hold the highest seats of power; high-ranking demon spirits that have held their seats of power since ancient times.*

The **second** category is called "powers," which is the Greek word *exousias.* This pictures *those who have received license to do whatever they wish wherever they desire to do it.*

The **third** classification Paul talked about is "rulers of the darkness of this world." This is the translation of the Greek word *kosmokratoras.* It is a compound of the word *kosmos*, which describes *something that is arranged or put in order*, and the word *kratos*, which means *power.* When the two words are joined to form *kosmokratoras*, it means *rulers; power that is arranged or disciplined; orderly power and troops.* This word lets us know that Satan has highly organized forces. He is very serious in his efforts to take us down.

The **fourth** group of enemy forces that comes against us is called "spiritual wickedness in high places." The word "wickedness" is the Greek word *poneria*, which describes *iniquity.* It pictures *something wicked, malevolent, or insidious.* The phrase "high places" actually describes *our earthly atmosphere.* These evil forces don't live out in the cosmos; they traffic in the very air we breathe.

All of this meaning and imagery are what is packed in Ephesians 6:12. Keep in mind, this verse states that we are not wrestling against flesh and blood. In other words, behind the flesh and blood you can see, there are invisible spiritual entities orchestrating their attack against you. The temptation we often face is to fight against the flesh and blood we can see, but that is futile. We must turn our attention to the real source of the conflict — demonic spiritual forces.

Jesus Encountered Demonic Opposition in the Form of a Storm

A vivid example of spiritual opposition can be seen in the account of Jesus' crossing the Sea of Galilee with His disciples. Mark 4:35 and 37 says, "...When the even was come, he saith unto them, Let us pass over unto the other side.... And there arose a great storm of wind, and the waves beat into the ship, so that it was now full."

To understand the storm and the reason it came, we need to fast forward to what happened once Jesus made it to the other side of the sea. Mark 5:1-3 says, "And they came over unto the other side of the sea, into the country of the Gadarenes. And when he was come out of the ship, immediately there met him out of the tombs a man with an unclean spirit who had his dwelling among the tombs...."

As soon as Jesus stepped out of the boat, a demonized man who was literally living among the tombs ran toward Him. The Bible says the man was "with an unclean spirit." The Greek here actually says "a man in the grip of" or "a man in the control of" an unclean spirit. Thus, the man didn't have the evil spirit; *the evil spirit had the man.*

Matthew's gospel records that there were *two* men who came toward Jesus. Although the Scripture may seem to be conflicted, it isn't. Mark focused on the one man who was more severely demonized, and Matthew gave us the big picture of what took place that day. Looking at Matthew's account, it says, "...There met him [Jesus] two possessed with devils, coming out of the tombs, exceeding fierce, so that no man might pass by that way."

The word "way" is the Greek word *hodos*, which means *road.* There was a major road that ran along the eastern shore of the sea of Galilee. As a result of these demonized men terrorizing everyone who passed by, people became quite afraid to take this road.

He Was on the Brink of a Major Breakthrough

Jesus was aware of the situation and of the demoniacs who were wreaking havoc in the area. He had a plan to set these men free and thereby liberate the entire region. The enemy knew what would likely happen once Jesus made it to the area of the Gadarenes; He would deliver the demoniacs, and Satan would lose the demonic stronghold he'd had in the region. Therefore, Satan stirred up a storm to try to stop the Lord.

Interestingly, the Bible says "there arose" a great storm of wind. The words "there arose" is translated from the Greek word *ginomai*, and it pictures *something that takes one off guard or by surprise; something unexpected; to happen (suddenly), or to come into being.*

There was nothing natural about this storm. It took Jesus and the disciples totally by surprise. It was a demonic attack designed to derail Jesus from accomplishing His mission. He was on the brink of a major breakthrough when, *suddenly*, He and His disciples were faced with a *ginomai* moment.

If you're under an attack right now, it is likely a sign that you are right on the edge of one of the greatest breakthroughs you've ever had in your life. Although the devil is not all-knowing, he can sense the strong possibility of something powerful about to happen in your life. Thus He is trying to stop you from experiencing it. But he cannot keep you from what the Lord has for you. As you continue to trust Him and move in the direction He called you, you will make it to the other side.

STUDY QUESTIONS

> **Study to shew thyself approved unto God, a workman that needeth not to be ashamed, rightly dividing the word of truth.**
> **— 2 Timothy 2:15**

1. After hearing the history and the Greek meaning of the word "wrestle" and its connection with the *palaestra* — the House of Combat — how has your understanding of the spiritual fight you're in expanded and become clearer?

2. According to Ephesians 6:12, there are at least four levels of evil forces we are up against. In your own words, briefly describe each of them. What does the fact that Satan has highly organized forces say to you personally? Does this concern you, or does it cause you to rise up determined to exercise your God-given authority in Christ?

PRACTICAL APPLICATION

> **But be ye doers of the word, and not hearers only, deceiving your own selves.**
> **—James 1:22**

1. Rick shared an example from his life about going through a financial storm just before a major breakthrough in his and Denise's life. In what ways can you personally identify with his story?

2. Ephesians 6:12 (*NLT*) says, "For we are not fighting against people made of flesh and blood, but against the evil rulers and authorities of the unseen world...." Be honest. Have you been fighting against people? Have you been lashing out at family members, coworkers, neighbors, or people in authority because of the undesirable circumstances in which you find yourself? How does this lesson help you see your situation and these people in a different light?

LESSON 2

TOPIC

Why and When
Spiritual Attacks Come

SCRIPTURES

1. **Mark 4:35-41** — And the same day, when the even was come, he saith unto them, Let us pass over unto the other side. And when they had sent away the multitude, they took him even as he was in the ship. And there were also with him other little ships. And there arose a great storm of wind, and the waves beat into the ship, so that it was now full. And he was in the hinder part of the ship, asleep on a pillow: and they awake him, and say unto him, Master, carest thou not that we perish? And he arose, and rebuked the wind, and said unto the sea, Peace, be still. And the wind ceased, and there was a great calm. And he said unto them, Why are ye so fearful? how is it that ye have no faith? And they feared exceedingly, and said one to another, What manner of man is this, that even the wind and the sea obey him?

2. **Mark 5:1-5** — And they came over unto the other side of the sea, into the country of the Gadarenes. And when he was come out of the ship, immediately there met him out of the tombs a man with an unclean spirit who had his dwelling among the tombs; and no man could bind him, no, not with chains Because that he had been often bound with fetters and chains, and the chains had been plucked asunder by him, and the fetters broken in pieces: neither could any man tame him. And always, night and day, he was in the mountains, and in the tombs, crying, and cutting himself with stones.

3. **Matthew 8:28** — And when he was come to the other side into the country of the Gergesenes, there met him two possessed with devils, coming out of the tombs, exceeding fierce, so that no man might pass by that way.

GREEK WORDS

1. "met" — ὑπαντάω (*hupantao*): to meet; in context, pictures a hostile confrontation
2. "exceeding fierce" — χαλεπός (*chalepos*): treacherous; high-risk; harmful; pictures a situation of jeopardy or something that could potentially harm you
3. "there arose" — γίνομαι (*ginomai*): pictures something that takes one off guard or by surprise; something unexpected; to happen (suddenly) or to come into being
4. "great" — μεγάλη (*megale*): unusually large; enormous
5. "wind" — λαῖλαψ (*lailaps*): turbulence in the atmosphere; a force that is felt but is not seen
6. "beat into" — ἐπιβάλλω (*epiballo*): to pick up and throw over and against
7. "waves" — κύματα (*kumata*): one succession of waves after another; this was an onslaught of nonstop waves

SYNOPSIS

After a long day of ministry, Jesus and His disciples boarded a boat and set sail for the region of the Gadarenes on the other side of the Sea of Galilee. Jesus had business to attend to — two people were being tortured by unclean spirits and desperately needed to be set free. While Jesus was en route, a huge windstorm suddenly arose and threatened to capsize the ship with the disciples in it. Although many of the men on board were veteran fishermen, they had never experienced a disturbance with such turbulence. If a natural storm had been brewing that night, they would have known and not ventured out. But this was no ordinary storm. It was a supernatural tempest stirred up by Satan in an effort to prevent Jesus from bringing freedom and deliverance to those in bondage "on the other side."

The emphasis of this lesson:

Spiritual attacks often come just before a major breakthrough. Satan will do all he can to prevent your progress. Nevertheless, God has anointed you to destroy the works of the devil.

A Mighty Miracle Was Waiting on the Other Side

Jesus and His disciples were on the brink of seeing an amazing deliverance. Mark 5:1-3 says, "They came over unto the other side of the sea, into the country of the Gadarenes. And when he was come out of the ship, immediately there met him out of the tombs a man with an unclean spirit who had his dwelling among the tombs...." Matthew's gospel records that there were *two* demonized men. Although the accounts seem to be in conflict, they aren't. Mark focused on the man who was in a worse condition, and Matthew presented the big picture of what took place.

The demonized men who "met" Jesus were literally living in the midst of the tombs. The word "met" in verse 2 is the Greek word *hupantao*, which is *a military term that describes a hostile confrontation*. The demons living in these men were not happy that Jesus showed up. Matthew 8:28 describes these evil spirits as "exceeding fierce," which is the Greek word *chalepos*, meaning *treacherous; high-risk; harmful*. It pictures *a situation of jeopardy or something that could potentially harm you*.

The people in the region understood that the environment where the demoniacs lived was harmful and treacherous. In fact, when people traveled on the major roadway that ran through the area, the demoniacs would lunge at and attack them as they passed by. The entire eastern side of the Sea of Galilee became terrorized by the evil spirits operating through these men.

Nevertheless, once Jesus arrived on the scene, He delivered these two tormented souls from the power of Satan and brought peace to the region in the process (*see* Mark 5:1-15). But before Jesus could get there and effectively carry out His mission, He and His disciples encountered major interference from the enemy.

Jesus and the Disciples Experienced an Unexpected Storm

Mark 4:35-37 says, "And the same day, when the even was come, he [Jesus] saith unto them, Let us pass over unto the other side. And when they had sent away the multitude, they took him even as he was in the ship. And there were also with him other little ships. And there arose a great storm of wind, and the waves beat into the ship, so that it was now full."

The words "there arose" in verse 37 is the Greek word *ginomai*, which means *something unexpected; to happen (suddenly), or to come into being*. It pictures *something that takes one off guard or by surprise*. Remember, the majority of Jesus' disciples were professional fishermen, and they knew the weather patterns of Galilee very well. If there had been a natural storm brewing that night, they would have known it and stayed in port. By using the word *ginomai*, the Holy Spirit is telling us that this storm *took them completely off guard and by surprise*. It came out of nowhere and was the last thing they anticipated.

The Bible says it was a "great" storm. The word "great" is the Greek word *megale*, which describes *something unusually large; enormous*. In other words, this storm was beyond anything they had ever seen. It was an enormous storm of "wind," which in Greek is the word *lailaps*, and it describes *turbulence in the atmosphere; a force that is felt, but it is not seen*.

If you have been on an airplane, you have likely experienced turbulence. The greater the turbulence, the more unnerved and disturbed you probably felt. Although you can't touch wind, you can certainly feel its effects. What's interesting is that there is no indication of any rain with this storm Jesus and His disciples found themselves in — just wind (*lailaps*).

It's possible that the disciples tried to explain the origin of the storm that night using their knowledge and experience of the sea and weather patterns. They knew that there were mountains just to the north of the Sea of Galilee. If the atmospheric conditions abruptly changed, the winds could begin surging down those mountains onto the sea, slapping the water's surface with such force that it would create great waves. But that was not what the disciples were experiencing that night.

Jesus and His men were dealing with an invisible force that had come to assault them because they were heading to the region of the Gadarenes to cast the demons out of the demoniacs. This windstorm was the devil's attempt to capsize the boat and drown Jesus and the disciples.

Wave After Wave Beat Into the Ship

The Bible goes on to say that "...the waves beat into the ship, so that it was now full" (Mark 4:37). The phrase "beat into" is the Greek word *epiballo*, which is a compound of the word *epi*, meaning *over*, and the word *ballo*, meaning *to throw, to cast*, or *to hurl*. When these two words come together to form *epiballo*, it is normally the picture of *a person who picks something up and throws it over and against something else*. In context here, it describes *an entity or personality that is picking up the waves of the sea and hurling them against the ship*.

The word "waves" is also significant. It is the Greek word *kumata*, and it describes *one succession of waves after another*. This was *an onslaught of nonstop waves*. The use of this word tells us that what the disciples were dealing with that night looked and felt like a hopeless situation. There seemed to be no end to the series of monstrous waves coming at them.

If the storm had been an ordinary one, the waves would have likely been moving in one direction. But on this particular night, Jesus and His disciples had become a target out in the middle of the Sea of Galilee. An enormous storm of turbulence unlike they had ever encountered before began hurling wave after wave at them from all directions. Again, Jesus was on the brink of a breakthrough, and the devil was trying to stop Him.

Deal With the *Source* of the Storm, Not Its Symptoms

In the next few lessons, we're going to see that the disciples began bailing water and binding the waves. However, the waves were not the problem. The problem was *the wind*.

By dealing with the waves, the disciples were merely dealing with the *symptoms*. The waves were the tangible, "flesh-and-blood" element that they could see. Unfortunately, as soon as they dealt with one wave, there was another wave immediately behind it — and another one followed by another one followed by another one.

When you come under a satanic assault, you can either surrender to it or stand up and take authority over it. The devil wants you to focus on the symptoms of your situation. He knows that he can just keep sending you more and more symptoms, and as long as you are focused on the symptoms, he will keep you distracted and eventually exhaust you in the process. You have to look beyond the symptoms to the source of the storm. In the disciples' case, it was the wind. Once Jesus stood up and addressed this invisible force, the symptoms ceased, and the same thing will happen in your life when you stand up and take authority over the enemy. He is the source behind the undesirable symptoms you're facing.

STUDY QUESTIONS

Study to shew thyself approved unto God, a workman that needeth not to be ashamed, rightly dividing the word of truth.
— 2 Timothy 2:15

1. Satan and his demonic forces are identified by Jesus in John 10:10 as the *thief.* By understanding how the thief works, you can determine the source of the circumstances you are experiencing. Carefully read this verse and identify the characteristics of Satan's activity and then describe Jesus' activity in your life.

2. Christ's death and resurrection not only provides you with forgiveness for your sins, but also victory over the enemy. Meditate on the truth found in Luke 10:19; John 16:33; Colossians 2:15; and Psalm 44:5-8. How do these declarations invigorate your faith?

PRACTICAL APPLICATION

But be ye doers of the word, and not hearers only,
deceiving your own selves.
— James 1:22

The phrase "there arose" in Mark 4:37 is the Greek word *ginomai*, which pictures *something that takes one off guard or by surprise; something totally unexpected.* The storm of wind that Jesus and the disciples experienced was a *ginomai* moment for them.

1. More than likely, you have experienced a *ginomai* moment in your life. Take time to briefly describe one of the most memorable *ginomai* moments you have faced.

2. What were the "flesh and blood" symptoms that came against you?
3. What breakthrough was the enemy trying to keep you from experiencing?
4. How did the Lord deliver you from the storm you were in?

TOPIC

Dealing With Faithless Thoughts When You're Under Attack

SCRIPTURES

1. **Matthew 8:28** — And when he was come to the other side into the country of the Gergesenes, there met him two possessed with devils, coming out of the tombs, exceeding fierce, so that no man might pass by that way.
2. **Mark 4:35, 37-39** — And the same day, when the even was come, he saith unto them, Let us pass over unto the other side. And there arose a great storm of wind, and the waves beat into the ship, so that it was now full. And he was in the hinder part of the ship, asleep on a pillow: and they awake him, and say unto him, Master, carest thou not that we perish? And he arose, and rebuked the wind, and said unto the sea, Peace, be still. And the wind ceased, and there was a great calm.
3. **Ephesians 6:12** — For we wrestle not against flesh and blood, but against principalities, against powers, against the rulers of the darkness of this world, against spiritual wickedness in high places.

GREEK WORDS

1. "exceeding fierce" — χαλεπός (*chalepos*): treacherous; high-risk; harmful; pictures a situation of jeopardy or something that could potentially harm you
2. "there arose" — γίνομαι (*ginomai*): pictures something that takes one off guard or by surprise; something unexpected; to happen (suddenly) or to come into being

3. "great" — **μεγάλη** (*megale*): unusually large; enormous
4. "wind" — **λαῖλαψ** (*lailaps*): turbulence in the atmosphere; a force that is felt but not seen
5. "beat into" — **ἐπιβάλλω** (*epiballo*): to pick up and throw over and against
6. "awake" — **ἐγείρω** (*egeiro*): to raise up; the same root for the word "resurrection"
7. "perish" — **ἀπόλλυμι** (*apollumi*): to destroy; pictures something utterly undone, unraveled, coming apart, or coming to pieces

SYNOPSIS

In obedience to Jesus' command, the disciples boarded a ship with Him and set sail for the country of the Gadarenes. While en route, a mighty storm arose, which was totally unexpected and caught them completely off guard. Wave after wave beat against their ship from every direction, placing the disciples in a feverish panic. Again and again, they bailed water while binding the waves. How long this went on the Bible doesn't say. Nevertheless, when they could take no more, they woke Jesus from His sleep and demanded that He do something about their perilous situation.

The emphasis of this lesson:

Just as Jesus had called His disciples to cross to the other side of the sea, He has called you to a specific destiny. Don't give in to fear when you're under attack. You're going to make it!

Jesus Was on a Mission To Bring Deliverance

In our previous lessons, we learned that once Jesus and His disciples successfully made it to the region of the Gadarenes, He was immediately met by two demonized men who were "exceeding fierce" (*see* Matthew 8:28). This phrase "exceeding fierce" is the Greek word *chalepos* — a word that is only used in one other place in the New Testament. *Chalepos* means *treacherous; high-risk; harmful*. It pictures *a situation of jeopardy or something that could potentially harm you*. It is translated as the word "perilous" in Second Timothy 3:1, and it always carries the idea of *peril, danger, risk, harm*, and *destruction*.

The Bible says the demonized men were so dangerous "…that no man might pass by that way" (Matthew 8:28). The word "way" is the Greek word *hodos*, which describes *a road*. During that time, there was a major roadway parallel to the Sea of Galilee that was used by many travelers. In time, however, the threatening actions of these demonized men generated such fear in the people that they stopped traveling on that road.

Once Jesus learned of the torment these men were enduring and the terror that gripped the people because of the demoniacs, He traveled to deliver the demoniacs and set the region free from the spirit of fear. That is what He and His disciples were en route to do the night Jesus was crossing the Sea of Galilee.

The Enemy Tried To Stop Jesus by Stirring Up a Storm

Mark 4:37 says, "And there arose a great storm of wind, and the waves beat into the ship, so that it was now full." The phrase "there arose" is the Greek word *ginomai*, which we learned about in the previous lessons. It means *to happen (suddenly) or to come into being.* It is something *unexpected* and pictures something that *takes one off guard or by surprise.*

As noted before, most of the men with Jesus were fishermen by profession. They had spent countless hours on the water and knew well the weather of the region. If a natural storm had been brewing that evening, these men would have recognized the telltale signs and avoided going out on the water altogether. But there was nothing natural about this storm.

By using the word *ginomai* — translated here as "there arose" — it was as if the disciples were saying, "We have no idea where this storm came from. It was the last thing we would have anticipated. It completely took us off guard and by surprise."

Verse 37 also says that it was a "great storm of wind." The word "great" is the word *megale*, which describes *something unusually large or enormous.* These experienced seamen had seen many storms, but they had never seen anything like *that* storm. Furthermore, it was not a rainstorm but a storm of "wind." The word "wind" is the Greek word *lailaps*, and it describes *turbulence in the atmosphere; a force that is felt, but it is not seen.*

It was this wind that created "waves," which "beat into the ship." The word "waves" is the Greek word *kumata*, and it describes *a succession of nonstop waves.* As far as the disciples could see, there was one wave after another after another coming toward their boat from all directions.

The phrase "beat into" is the Greek word *epiballo*, which means *to pick up and throw over and against*. This word never describes the activity of nature. Instead, it describes what a person or an entity does. By using the word *epiballo*, the Holy Spirit is letting us know that *an invisible entity was picking up the waves of the sea and hurling them over and against the ship*.

Jesus and His disciples became the target of the enemy. Wave after wave after wave from all directions were being picked up and hurled at them as they attempted to make their way across the Sea of Galilee to the region of the Gadarenes. The onslaught was so great that the ship had begun to fill with water.

Jesus and His Disciples Reacted Very Differently

Where was Jesus when this great windstorm suddenly arose? Mark 4:38 says, "And he was in the hinder part of the ship, asleep on a pillow...." Interestingly, the word "pillow" is important, as it describes the place and position in which Jesus was sleeping. In Greek, this word "pillow" describes *a small cushion that fit right up in the corner of the ship*, and it indicates that Jesus was curled up in a tight position getting some enjoyable sleep.

Meanwhile, the disciples were frantically binding waves and bailing water, trying desperately to survive the extreme turbulence. Although they were terrorized by the wind-whipped waters, Jesus was totally at peace — totally secure in the knowledge that they would make it to the other side. The rocking of the boat served only to lull Him to sleep.

When the weary disciples could take no more, "...they awake him, and say unto him, Master, carest thou not that we perish?" The word "awake" in this verse is the same root word for "resurrection." Thus when the Bible says, "They awake Him," it means they didn't politely and gently wake Jesus from sleep! Instead, they jerked Him off the pillow so abruptly, it appeared as if He was being resurrected from the dead!

In desperation they cried, "Master, carest thou not that we perish?" The word "perish" is the Greek word *apollumi*, which is the compound of two words: the word *apo* means *away from*, and the word *lumi*, which is from the word *luo*, means *to undo* or *to unloose*. When the words *apo* and *lumi* are combined to form *apollumi*, it means *to destroy*. It pictures *something utterly undone, unraveled, coming apart, or coming to pieces.* In this case, it was the disciples who were unraveled and coming apart at the seams.

'Lord, Teacher, Master'

The way we respond when trouble first hits our lives is often very different than the way we respond to lingering problems that seem to have no end. Very often when we run into long, drawn-out difficulties, we begin to question God just as the disciples did.

A careful study of the storm on the Sea of Galilee recorded in the synoptic gospels — Matthew, Mark, and Luke — reveals that the disciples responded in three different ways. When they went to Jesus to wake Him up, they called Him *Lord, Teacher*, and *Master*. These three titles represent three different levels of faith.

Matthew 8:25 says, "His disciples came to him, and awoke him, saying *Lord*, save us: we perish." The word "Lord" here is the Greek word *Kurios*, and it means *Sovereign One who is in control.* When we are initially confronted with difficulty, we tend to address God as "Lord," which means we know and recognize that He is in control, and our faith is still holding strong. Although things are challenging, we confidently believe everything is going to work out and that the Lord is going to take care of us.

If problems persist, our faith level changes, and we begin calling out to Jesus like the disciples did in Mark 4:38, saying, "…Master, carest thou not that we perish?" The word "Master" here is the Greek word *didaskalos*, which means *teacher.* Essentially, we are still acknowledging that Jesus is Lord and in control, but because the difficulties haven't gone away, we think that God is somehow trying *to teach* us something through the situation.

Then when trials and troubles continue to drag on and we have had all the "teaching" we can take, we begin to cry out to God like the disciples did in Luke 8:24, saying, "…Master, master, we perish…." In this verse, the word "Master" is the Greek word *epistates*, which is a compound of the words *epi*, meaning *upon*, and *states*, meaning *to stand.* When these two words are combined to form the word *epistates*, it means, "Master, please get on the spot and do something in this moment. We're calling on You to act right here, right now!"

The truth is, when you're in the middle of a storm in the "midnight hour" of your life and you're about to be capsized and drowned like the disciples were, it is not the time God is trying to "teach" you something. The intensity of the situation doesn't create a good environment for learning! If you find yourself in that position, cry out to Jesus in to intervene and deliver you. *Let Him teach you later.*

After the Disciples Had a Pity-Party, Jesus Had Mercy on Them and Delivered Them!

Another interesting thing to note in Mark 4:38 is the phrase "carest thou not." In the Greek, this actually says, "Is there no care in You toward us?" In other words, the disciples moved into the realm of self-pity and began to have a pity party! If you have begun a pity party of your own, you need to know that that kind of attitude never improves the situation; it usually only serves to keep you in your situation longer.

In His mercy, Jesus heard the disciples' cry for help and moved into action. Mark 4:39 says, "And he arose, and rebuked the wind, and said unto the sea, Peace, be still. And the wind ceased, and there was a great calm."

For much of the night, the disciples had spent all their energy bailing water and fighting the waves. But Jesus stood up and addressed the root of the problem: the wind (*lailaps*, or *turbulence in the atmosphere*). He ignored the waves, which were only the *symptoms* of the problem, and dealt directly with the *source* of the problem — the spiritual entity stirring up the ghastly winds.

This leads us back to Ephesians 6:12, which says, "For we wrestle not against flesh and blood, but against principalities, against powers, against the rulers of the darkness of this world, against spiritual wickedness in high places." Like the disciples' problem, our struggle is not against flesh and blood (for example, "the waves"). Our fight is against an unseen entity. If you will trust God's Word, take a stand in faith, and invite Him into your situation, He will release His power to defeat the enemy on your behalf.

STUDY QUESTIONS

**Study to shew thyself approved unto God, a workman that
needeth not to be ashamed, rightly dividing the word of truth.
— 2 Timothy 2:15**

Have you ever felt like the disciples felt — totally undone and coming
apart at the seams in the midst of a storm, wondering if the Lord was
aware of what you were going through? If so, take a few moments to
reflect on the following verses. What do each of these promises from God
show you, and how do they encourage you and bring you hope?

1. Joshua 1:5,9 and Hebrews 13:5,6 show me the God _____
    _____.

2. Psalm 121 plainly states that God _____
    _____.

3. Isaiah 41:10-16 and 43:1,2 help me to realize that God _____
    _____.

4. Numbers 23:19; Deuteronomy 7:9; and 1 Kings 8:56 reveal that God
    _____.

PRACTICAL APPLICATION

**But be ye doers of the word, and not hearers only,
deceiving your own selves.
— James 1:22**

1. Jesus and His disciples were heading to the area of the Gadarenes to
    bring deliverance to the demonized men and freedom to the region.
    This was their assignment. Do you know what your present assign-
    ment is that the devil is trying to keep you from fulfilling? If so, take a
    moment to briefly describe it.

2. If you don't know where God is taking you or what He is presently
    asking you to do, take a moment to pause and pray. Ask Him, "Lord,
    why is the enemy fighting me so hard? What are You asking me to
    do? If You have already told me, please remind me and give me Your
    strength to obediently carry out the assignment. In Jesus' name."

TOPIC

Taking Authority Over the Invisible Realm

SCRIPTURES

1. **Mark 4:35, 37-41** — And the same day, when the even was come, he saith unto them, Let us pass over unto the other side. And there arose a great storm of wind, and the waves beat into the ship, so that it was now full. And he was in the hinder part of the ship, asleep on a pillow: and they awake him, and say unto him, Master, carest thou not that we perish? And he arose, and rebuked the wind, and said unto the sea, Peace, be still. And the wind ceased, and there was a great calm. And he said unto them, Why are ye so fearful? how is it that ye have no faith? And they feared exceedingly, and said one to another, What manner of man is this, that even the wind and the sea obey him?

GREEK WORDS

1. "there arose" — γίνομαι (*ginomai*): pictures something that takes one off guard or by surprise; something unexpected; to happen (suddenly) or to come into being

2. "great" — μεγάλη (*megale*): unusually large; enormous

3. "wind" — λαῖλαψ (*lailaps*): turbulence in the atmosphere; a force that is felt but not seen

4. "beat into" — ἐπιβάλλω (*epiballo*): to pick up and throw over and against

5. "perish" — ἀπόλλυμι (*apollumi*): to destroy; pictures something utterly undone, unraveled, coming apart, or coming to pieces

6. "rebuked" — ἐπιτιμάω (*epitimao*): an series of words meant to censure; to humiliate; to chide; to verbally assault

7. "wind" — ἄνεμος (*anemos*): in this context, a horrible storm

8. "ceased" — κοπάζω (*kopadzo*): to grow weary; pictures one so exhausted that he gives up the fight

SYNOPSIS

While Jesus and His disciples were en route to the area of the Gadarenes, they encountered opposition. A great storm of wind arose suddenly and unexpectedly, and the wind was so fierce, it created a bombardment of waves that began to beat against their boat. With great effort, the disciples bailed water from the ship and fought valiantly against the waves, but it was to no avail.

At that time, Jesus was asleep in the ship. When the disciples were exhausted from their efforts, they woke the Lord, and He rebuked the wind and the waves. Once He took authority over the wind — the force in the invisible realm that was behind the problem — He then exercised authority over the waves, and they obeyed Him.

The emphasis of this lesson:

Instead of expending your energy fighting the *symptoms* of your problems, focus on and deal with the invisible realm like Jesus did. When you do, you will get supernatural results.

Suddenly, a Great Storm of Wind Arose

One evening after ministering to the multitudes all day, Jesus and His disciples got into a boat, and He told them, "…Let us pass over unto the other side…" (Mark 4:35). Verse 37 says, "And there arose a great storm of wind, and the waves beat into the ship, so that it was now full."

We've seen in previous lessons that the phrase "there arose" is the Greek word *ginomai*, and it describes *something that takes one off guard or by surprise; something unexpected.* When Jesus and the disciples started their journey, it appeared to be the perfect night for sailing. Many of the men with Him were professional fishermen who knew the water and the weather of the region like the back of their hands. If a natural storm had been brewing, they would have known it and stayed ashore. However, since the conditions were peaceful, they set out without a second thought.

Suddenly, out of nowhere, a great storm of wind arose (*ginomai*). It was the last thing they would have anticipated. The word "great" is the Greek word *megale*, and it describes *something unusually large or enormous.* The word "wind" is the Greek word *lailaps*, and it describes *turbulence in the atmosphere; a force that is felt but not seen.* The disciples could feel the effects of the turbulence, but they couldn't see the source or grab hold of it.

An Invisible Entity Was at Work

The great storm of wind created "waves" that "beat into" the ship. The word "waves" is the Greek word *kumata*, which describes *a succession of nonstop waves.* One wave after another after another began to "beat into" the ship. The phrase "beat into" in Greek is the word *epiballo*, which means *to pick up and throw over and against.* This word is used to describe something that a person or an entity does. In the context of this verse, it lets us know that an invisible force was picking up the waves and throwing them against the ship.

Jesus and His disciples had become a target of the enemy that night. They were on their way to the country of the Gadarenes to bring people deliverance and freedom, and Satan was trying to stop them from fulfilling their assignment. Again and again and again, the enemy picked up those waves and threw them against their boat.

For what could have been hours, the disciples fought the waves and bailed water from their vessel. Their focus was on the *symptoms* of the problem, which is exactly where Satan wanted it. Even if they had successfully defeated one wave, he could easily create another one and send it in their direction. His plan was to distract them and get them to expend all their energy and strength on fighting the symptoms and thereby wear themselves out.

Although it is always good to use your brain and do what you know to do to overcome the challenges you're facing, you can't overlook the supernatural element that may be involved in your situation. So if you're sick, go see the doctor and take the prescribed medication. If you're having trouble in your marriage, read a good book or seek out a godly counselor. However, if you are doing everything you know to do in the natural and there is no improvement in your circumstances, it may be that you're dealing with a supernatural problem. That is what Jesus and His disciples were dealing with on the Sea of Galilee that night.

The Disciples Cried Out to Jesus in Desperation

It's interesting to note where Jesus was when the disciples were wrestling with the waves. Mark 4:38 says, "And he was in the hinder part of the ship, asleep on a pillow...." After attempting to deal with the storm themselves — probably for several hours — verse 38 says, "...They awake him, and say unto him, Master, carest thou not that we perish?"

The word "Master" in this verse is the Greek word *epistates*. It is the compound of two words: *epi*, which means *upon*, and *states*, which means *to stand*. When the two words are joined to form the word *epistates*, it means *to be on the spot; to demand that one do something right here, right now*. When the disciples cried "Master," it was their urgent plea for Jesus to immediately come to their aid. It was as if they were saying, "Master, we're calling on You to act *right now!*"

When the disciples said, "Carest thou not that we perish?" it could literally be translated from the Greek as, "Is there no care in You toward us?" In other words, "Jesus, do You not see what we're going through here? Do you not feel what we're feeling?" These words clearly indicate that they had drifted into the realm of self-pity.

The word "perish" is also significant. It is the Greek word *apollumi*, which means *to destroy*. It pictures *something utterly undone, unraveled, coming apart, or coming to pieces*. Essentially, the disciples were crying out, "Lord, we are coming unraveled — we are coming to pieces and are about to lose it. We need You to come here right now, in this moment, and do something!"

The moment Jesus was compelled to come, He came, and He was not offended by their insistence. Likewise, if you call on the name of the Lord, He will respond to you. He is just waiting for you to act in faith and call upon His mighty name.

Jesus Humiliated the Demonic Forces

In the disciples' case, the Bible says, "And he [Jesus] arose, and rebuked the wind, and said unto the sea, Peace, be still. And the wind ceased, and there was a great calm" (Mark 4:39). Notice that the first thing Jesus did to bring change to the situation was *to rebuke the wind*. He ignored the waves and the water crashing into the boat and spoke directly to the turbulence in the atmosphere.

The word "rebuked" is the Greek word *epitimao*, and it doesn't describe just a single word; it describes a *series* of words related to a specific action. It is used 29 times in the New Testament, which helps us know exactly what it means. The word *epitimao* is *a series of words meant to censure; to humiliate; to chide; to verbally assault.* When the Bible says Jesus "rebuked" the wind, it doesn't mean He said, "I rebuke you, wind." On the contrary, Jesus literally had a conversation with the spirit realm and verbally assaulted the evil spirits causing the turbulence.

Keep in mind that when Lucifer was in Heaven, the iniquity of pride was found in his heart, and that is what caused him to be kicked out. His name was then changed to Satan, and all the evil spirits who do his bidding reflect his arrogant character. When Jesus dealt with the demonic forces causing the turbulence and trying to capsize the boat, He humiliated them and they fled the scene.

The same thing will happen when you choose to submit yourself to God and resist the devil — the enemy will flee (*see* James 4:7). The word "flee" in Greek means *to move one's feet as fast as one can.* If you will submit to God and properly resist the enemy, he will make a mad dash to get away from you quickly.

The Enemy Gave Up the Fight

After Jesus "rebuked" the wind, He said to the sea, "...Peace, be still..." (Mark 4:39). The rest of that verse says, "...And the wind ceased, and there was a great calm." Once Jesus had dealt with the spirit realm, dealing with the waves was simple. He didn't yell at the sea; He simply spoke to it and said, "Peace be still."

In Greek, the word "peace" is the word *siopao*, which describes *silence, muteness,* or *a hush.* Thus, a good translation of Jesus' command, "Peace, be still" would be that Jesus said to the waters, "*Shhh*...that's enough." Like a parent hushes an agitated child, Jesus hushed the waters, and they obeyed Him.

The Bible says that "the wind ceased." The word "ceased" is the Greek word *kopadzo*, which means *to grow weary.* It pictures one so exhausted that *he gives up the fight.* The invisible spiritual forces that were assailing Jesus and the disciples *gave up the fight* when the Lord spoke and took authority over them and the situation. And that is what will happen to you when you exercise your God-given authority over the enemy and the situation *you're* facing.

STUDY QUESTIONS

Study to shew thyself approved unto God, a workman that needeth not to be ashamed, rightly dividing the word of truth.
— 2 Timothy 2:15

Like Rick and Denise have experienced at times in the ministry God has called them to, many believers experience financial storms. The great news is that God is very mindful of you and well able to provide for all your needs as well as the needs of your family. Take a few minutes to meditate on these promises from God's Word. What is the Holy Spirit showing you personally in these passages? Write out the verse(s) that encourages you most and commit it to memory.

1. David's words in Psalm 34:9,10 and 84:11.
2. Jesus' words in Matthew 6:25-34.
3. Paul's words in Second Corinthians 9:8-11 and Philippians 4:19.

PRACTICAL APPLICATION

But be ye doers of the word, and not hearers only, deceiving your own selves.
— James 1:22

The word "rebuked" is the Greek word *epitimao*, and it describes *a series of words meant to censure; to humiliate; to chide; or to verbally assault.* When Jesus "rebuked" the wind, He literally had a conversation with the spirit realm and verbally assaulted the evil spirits causing the turbulence.

1. What problem has persisted in your life even though you have tried many natural remedies to get rid of it?
2. God wants you to "rebuke" the spirits in the invisible realm who are orchestrating the symptoms you're facing. Take time to pray and write *a series of words based on Scripture that will censure, humiliate, and verbally assault* the real enemy you're facing.
3. Now use the God-inspired declaration you just wrote and speak it out against the enemy (as often as needed until he gets the message and flees).

TOPIC

Learning To Exercise Christ-Given Authority

SCRIPTURES

1. **Mark 4:35,37-41** — And the same day, when the even was come, he saith unto them, Let us pass over unto the other side. And there arose a great storm of wind, and the waves beat into the ship, so that it was now full. And he was in the hinder part of the ship, asleep on a pillow: and they awake him, and say unto him, Master, carest thou not that we perish? And he arose, and rebuked the wind, and said unto the sea, Peace, be still. And the wind ceased, and there was a great calm. And he said unto them, Why are ye so fearful? how is it that ye have no faith? And they feared exceedingly, and said one to another, What manner of man is this, that even the wind and the sea obey him?

GREEK WORDS

1. "there arose" — γίνομαι (*ginomai*): pictures something that takes one off guard or by surprise; something unexpected; to happen (suddenly) or to come into being

2. "wind" — λαῖλαψ (*lailaps*): turbulence in the atmosphere; a force that is felt but not seen

3. "beat into" — ἐπιβάλλω (*epiballo*): to pick up and throw over and against

4. "awake" — ἐγείρω (*egeiro*): to raise up; the same root for the word "resurrection"

5. "perish" — ἀπόλλυμι (*apollumi*): to destroy; pictures something utterly undone, unraveled, coming apart, or coming to pieces

6. "rebuked" — ἐπιτιμάω (*epitimao*): a series of words meant to censure; to humiliate; to chide; to verbally assault

7. "ceased" — κοπάζω (*kopadzo*): to grow weary; pictures one so exhausted that he gives up the fight

8. "great" — μεγάλη (*megale*): unusually large; enormous

9. "fearful" — δειλοί (*deiloi*): cowardly or fearful; in context, behaving as cowards

10. "have" — ἔχω (*echo*): to hold; to possess; to have something in one's possession

11. "obey" — ὑπακούω (*hupakouo*): to attend to or to obey; pictures one in a subordinate position who listens to any commanding voice that exercises vocal authority over him

SYNOPSIS

The Sea of Galilee is a beautiful, picturesque place to be on a warm, sunny day. But it is a very undesirable place when a storm kicks up. Many of Jesus' disciples were veteran seamen and knew this to be true. They would never have ventured out on the water the night Jesus told them to cross over to the Gadarenes had they felt a storm was imminent. Nevertheless, when the tempest of turbulence suddenly arose that night, they witnessed firsthand how to exercise Christ-given authority over the unseen realm of the spirit.

The emphasis of this lesson:

Jesus exercised authority over the wind and the waves, and He has given you the same authority over all the power of the enemy. It's time to stand in faith, lift your voice, and release that authority.

In the last four lessons, we have carefully examined the biblical account of the disciples crossing the Sea of Galilee. Led by Jesus, they were on their way to the country of the Gadarenes to deliver the demoniacs from an infestation of demons and set the region free from the spirit of fear that had held them captive.

However, just as Jesus was on the brink of a major breakthrough in His ministry, suddenly, He and His disciples ran into major opposition. Mark 4:37 says, "And there arose a great storm of wind, and the waves beat into the ship, so that it was now full." Once more, let's look at the meanings of the key words in this passage.

A Quick Review of What We've Discovered

The phrase "there arose" is the Greek word *ginomai*, which describes *something that takes one off guard or by surprise; something unexpected; to*

happen (suddenly) or to come into being. The storm was a *ginomai* moment for the disciples.

The word "wind" is the Greek word *lailaps*, and it describes *turbulence in the atmosphere; a force that is felt but not seen.* This wasn't a rainstorm or thunderstorm. It was a windstorm generated by an invisible force working behind the scenes trying to stop the forward progress of Jesus and His men.

The word "waves" is the Greek word *kumata*, which denotes *a nonstop series of waves.* One wave after another after another beat into the ship that night.

The phrase "beat into" in Greek is the word *epiballo*, which means *to pick up and throw over and against.* Jesus and His disciples became a target that magnetically attracted the enemy's attack. The unseen spiritual forces were picking up wave after wave after wave and hurling them at the ship from every direction.

The disciples were overwhelmed. They had seen many storms, but nothing like the one they were experiencing that night. After exhausting themselves from bailing water and binding waves, they decided to go to Jesus and ask Him for help.

Jesus was asleep. Mark 4:38 says, "And he was in the hinder part of the ship, asleep on a pillow: and they awake him, and say unto him, Master, carest thou not that we perish?" The word "awake" is the Greek word *egeiro*, which means *to raise up.* It is the same root for the word "resurrection." In other words, the disciples didn't gently nudge Jesus to wake Him up. They *jerked* Him out of His sleep while yelling, "Master, carest thou not that we perish?"

The word "Master" is the Greek word *epistates*. It is a compound of the words *epi*, which means *upon*, and the word *states*, which means *to stand.* When the two words are combined to form the word *epistates*, it is the equivalent of saying, "Lord, be on the spot right now! Please come here this very moment and exercise Your authority over this situation."

The word "perish" in Mark 4:38 is the Greek word *apollumi*. It is a compound of the words *apo*, meaning *to be undone or remove*, and the word *lumi*, which is from the word *luo*, meaning *to loosen; to become relaxed.* When the words *apo* and *lumi* are joined to form the word *apollumi*, it pictures *something utterly undone, unraveled, coming apart, or coming to* *pieces.* Not only was the situation unraveling, but the disciples themselves were unraveling and spiraling out of control.

Jesus arose and rebuked the wind (*see* Mark 4:39). As we saw in our last lesson, the word "rebuked" is the Greek word *epitimao,* and it appears 29 times in the New Testament. It is a compound of two words: the word *epi,* which in this verse means *against,* and the word *timao,* which is the word for *honor.* When the two words are combined to form the word *epitimao,* it describes *a series of words meant to censure; to humiliate; to chide; to verbally assault.*

The word "wind" in verse 39 is again the Greek word *lailaps,* which signifies *turbulence in the atmosphere.* It was the "wind" (*lailaps*) to which Jesus immediately directed His attention. He knew that their problem was not the waves. It was the spiritual forces assaulting them. So instead of expending His energy trying to deal with the symptoms, He began speaking to the storm's source — the spirit realm. He *dishonored, humiliated, and verbally assaulted* the evil spirits.

Jesus knew the best way to deal with Satan. He was there when Lucifer got kicked out of Heaven. Pride was Satan's downfall. Thus, humiliation was *and still is* the most effective method to make him and his cohorts flee. James 4:7 says, "Submit yourselves therefore to God. Resist the devil, and he will flee from you." The word "flee" means *to move your feet as fast as you can.* Satan will make a dash and flee from you when you stand up and resist him while in submission to God.

After rebuking the wind, Jesus spoke to the sea. Mark 4:39 says, "…And [Jesus] said unto the sea, Peace, be still. And the wind ceased, and there was a great calm." Jesus didn't yell or repeatedly scream at the problem. He simply said, "Peace be still." The word "peace" is the Greek word *siopao,* which means *silence, muteness,* or *a hush.* Therefore, when Jesus spoke "Peace be still," it was as if He said to the waters, "*Shhh…*that's enough."

The Bible says that "the wind ceased." The word "ceased" is the Greek word *kopadzo,* which means *to grow weary.* It is a picture of one so exhausted that he *gives up the fight.* That person has struggled and strained and done his best, and now he is totally spent. Hence, when the Scripture says that the wind "ceased," it means the evil spirits in the invisible realm gave up the fight and went away.

The results of their surrender were amazing. Verse 39 says, "…There was a great calm." The word "great" is the Greek word *megale,* which means *unusually large; enormous*. It's the same word used in verse 37 to describe the "great" storm of wind that arose. The night began with a "great" storm of wind, but when Jesus was finished rebuking the wind, it ended with a "great" calm. This tells us that whatever problems the devil brings, you can count on Jesus matching it with the same intensity of good.

Jesus addressed His disciples. As a great calm settled on the waters, the Lord turned to His disciples and said to them, "…Why are ye so fearful? how is it that ye have no faith?" (Mark 4:40) The word "fearful" in Greek is the word *deiloi*, which means *cowardly or fearful*. Cowards hide, shrink in fear, and choose not to face their enemy. That is how the disciples were behaving. So, in effect, Jesus said, "Why are you behaving like cowards?"

He then added, "How is it that ye have no faith?" The word "have" is the Greek word *echo*, which means *to hold; to possess; to have something in one's possession*. Here, Jesus was literally saying, "You have faith. It is in your possession. Why are you acting like you don't have it? Why are you not using it?"

In response to Jesus' questions, the Bible says, "They feared exceedingly, and said one to another…" (Mark 4:40). The Greek meaning here denotes that the men began turning to each other and were talking among themselves while they were in the boat, saying "…What manner of man is this, that even the wind and the sea obey him?"

The word "obey" is the Greek word *hupakouo*. It is a compound of two words: the word *hupo*, which means *to be under, as to be in subjection to someone*, and the word *akouo*, which means *I hear*. It is where we get the word "acoustics." When the words *hupo* and *akouo* are compounded to form the word *hupakouo*, it means *to attend to or to obey*. It pictures *one in a subordinate position who listens to any commanding voice that exercises vocal authority over him*.

Within the word *hupakouo* — translated hear as *obey* — is the idea of *submission* and *listening*. In effect, it means that if you will speak to the spirit realm in your Christ-given authority, it will listen to you (*akouo*), and it will submit and fall in line (*hupo*). However, if you don't speak and exercise your authority, the evil spirits will push you around.

Friend, you have everything you need to deal with any evil spirit that is harassing you. Just as the disciples had been given faith and authority, you have been given faith and authority in Jesus Christ (*see* Luke 10:19). Don't shrink back in fear and allow the enemy to push you around. Rise to the occasion and in faith begin to lift your voice and release your authority! Victory is yours in Jesus' name!

STUDY QUESTIONS

Study to shew thyself approved unto God, a workman that needeth not to be ashamed, rightly dividing the word of truth.
— 2 Timothy 2:15

Romans 12:3 says, "...God hath dealt to every man the measure of faith." Ephesians 2:8 and 9 confirms this saying, "...It is the gift of God: not of works, lest any man should boast."

1. What is faith and how valuable is it? See God's answer to this in Hebrews 11:1,6 and First John 5:4.
2. Have you ever felt that your faith was not enough? Read how Jesus answered your concern in Luke 17:5,6 (*see* also Matthew17:20,21; Mark 11:22,23).
3. Have you wondered if there was something you could do to see your faith grow? Paul answers this question in Romans 10:17. Meditate on this verse and write about how faith grows.

PRACTICAL APPLICATION

But be ye doers of the word, and not hearers only, deceiving your own selves.
—James 1:22

Some of the storms we face in life seem very overwhelming. In times like these, it is good to reach out to a trusted friend who can join his faith with yours in prayer. Indeed, there is exponential power in the prayer of agreement.

1. Who can you turn to in a time of need to agree with in prayer?
2. When you're united in your request to God, what did Jesus say you can expect to happen? (*See* Matthew 18:18-20.)
3. In light of the symptoms that the enemy has stirred up to distract you, what specifically do you need to stand up and take authority over in the spirit realm?

A Prayer To Receive Salvation

If you've never received Jesus as your Savior and Lord, now is the time for you to experience the new life Jesus wants to give you! To receive God's gift of salvation that can be obtained through Jesus alone, pray this prayer from your heart:

> *Jesus, I repent of my sin and receive You as my Savior and Lord. Wash away my sin with Your precious blood and make me completely new. I thank You that my sin is removed, and Satan no longer has any right to lay claim on me. Through Your empowering grace, I faithfully promise that I will serve You as my Lord for the rest of my life.*

If you just prayed this prayer of salvation, you are born again! You are a brand-new creation in Christ! Would you please let us know of your decision by going to **renner.org/salvation**? We would love to connect with you and pray for you as you begin your new life in Christ.

Scriptures for further study: John 3:16; John 14:6; Acts 4:12; Ephesians 1:7; Hebrews 10:19,20; 1 Peter 1:18,19; Romans 10:9,10; Colossians 1:13; 2 Corinthians 5:17; Romans 6:4; 1 Peter 1:3

Notes

_____

_____

_____

_____

_____

_____

_____

_____

_____

_____

_____

_____

_____

_____

_____

_____

_____

_____

_____

_____

_____

_____

_____

_____

_____

_____

_____

_____

CLAIM YOUR FREE RESOURCE!

As a way of introducing you further to the teaching ministry of Rick Renner, we would like to send you FREE of charge his teaching, "How To Receive a Miraculous Touch From God" on CD or as an MP3 download.

In His earthly ministry, Jesus commonly healed *all* who were sick of *all* their diseases. In this profound message, learn about the manifold dimensions of Christ's wisdom, goodness, power, and love toward all humanity who came to Him in faith with their needs.

☑ **YES, I want to receive Rick Renner's monthly teaching letter!**

Simply scan the QR code to claim this resource or go to:
renner.org/claim-your-free-offer

Connect WITH US!